Advanced Praise for *Wealth Without Wall Street: A Main Street Guide to Making Money*

"Don McNay is an original, provocative voice taking on all of those who would get rich off our ignorance and feelings of financial desperation."
—Gary Rivlin, Newsweek/Daily Beast, author of *BROKE, USA*

"Don McNay understands money ... how to make it and, better yet, how to hang onto it. Read his book. It goes down easy, and it will do you a world of good."
—Ed McClanahan, author of *The Natural Man, Famous People I Have Known* and other books

"At last, a road atlas to wealth for those of us who don't like driving on Wall Street."
—Byron Crawford, award-winning columnist, author, broadcaster, and member of the Kentucky Journalism Hall of Fame

*"*Wealth Without Wall Street *offers plainspoken advice from financial columnist and expert Don McNay. His guidebook is a wealth-building road map based on his long-time experience as a respected financial consultant."*
—Suzette Martinez Standring, syndicated columnist, GateHouse News Service

"Don McNay combines deep understanding of his subjects with straight-forward, clear writing and plain ol' common sense to help all of us think more clearly about the big issues."

—Judy Clabes, editor, KyForward.com; former editor, The Kentucky Post; member of the Kentucky Journalism Hall of Fame

"Don McNay has nailed it. In our changing economic climate this is a must-read. In a realistic way, he has taken a complicated subject and made it easy to understand."

—Jim LaBarbara, member of the Radio/Television Broadcasters Hall of Fame, author of *The Music Professor, a Memoir*

"Don understands money, but his real strength is understanding people. He has real insight into what motivates the players and he explains it well to my audience. He's one of my favorite guests."

—Joe Elliott, Louisville, Kentucky; The Joe Elliott Show

"You don't have to study the labor disputes in professional sports, the misdeeds in college sports, or the politics in Washington for very long to see there's a shortage of common sense. That's exactly what I found when I started reading Don McNay's columns several years ago. We brought him on our radio show at that time to talk about financial issues in a way that connected with people more than someone looking to come up with a great sound bite."

—Tom Leach, radio host and two-time winner of the Eclipse Award for broadcasting excellence

"Don McNay explains Wall Street in a way that's both relevant and readable. Don't be intimidated by his 'structured settlement consultant' title. Reading Don's work is like having a conversation with an old friend; an old friend who's as proud of his rock n' roll record collection as he is of his investment portfolio".

—Samantha Swindler, publisher and editor, Tillamook Headlight-Herald, Tillamook, Oregon; winner of the 2010 Tom and Pat Gish Award for courage, integrity, and tenacity in rural journalism

"Thank goodness the characters in my books have never gone to Don McNay for financial advice. It's nearly impossible to create conflict in characters who are prospering. Read Wealth Without Wall Street *or you may end up in one of my novels."*

—Rick Robinson, 2010 Independent Author of the Year for the political thriller *Manifest Destiny*

"Don McNay doesn't try to impress you with his knowledge; he cuts through all the Wall Street hyperbole and breaks it down into what matters most, dollars and 'sense.' His no-nonsense approach to money provides sensible, practical advice in a humorous fashion. He's one of my favorite guests, and I always learn something new."

—Neil Middleton, award-winning journalist, vice president of news WYMT-TV

"When Don McNay shares his remarkable experience and astute advice, as he does in Wealth Without Wall Street, *you can take it to the bank— literally. And you will be glad you did."*

—O. Leonard (Len) Press, founder, Kentucky Educational Television

"I have been a big fan of Don McNay's for many years. Don's writing style is real pragmatic without the hyperbole. He writes for the everyday person in a style that's fun to read, with very sharp insights for everyday investors. Don has not been afraid to call out the big institutions, while sharing the benefits of terrific opportunities right in our own backyards. This is a great read."

—Keith Yarber, owner/founder, Tops In Lex

Wealth Without Wall Street

Previous books by Don McNay:

Son of a Son of a Gambler:
Winners, Losers and What to Do When You Win the Lottery

The Unbridled World of Ernie Fletcher

Wealth Without Wall Street

A Main Street Guide to Making Money

By

Don McNay, CLU, ChFC, MSFS, CSSC

RRP International LLC

978-0-9793644-8-8 (paperback)

978-0-9793644-7-1 (hardback)

RRP International LLC
316 Carriage Hill Ct.
Richmond, Ky. 40475

Publisher Number: 6032383

Since the time that I dedicated my previous two books, my granddaughter, Adelaide Ruth Bigler, has come into the world. She brings me joy and hope for a bright future. She also is adorably cute and can cause her grandpa to throw away his high-minded wisdom about disciplined spending.

Nearly fifty years ago, Dr. Al Smith overcame alcoholism to become one of Kentucky's most important and influential figures. He is my friend, mentor, role model, and inspiration.

At age eighty-four, he continues to make a tremendous impact on Kentucky and the world.

I want to be Al when I grow up.

My fiancée, Karen Thomas, has shown me that being in a loving relationship is the true key to happiness. The story of how we became engaged is worth reading at http://www.huffingtonpost.com/don-mcnay/im-getting-married-despit_b_893860.html

I dedicate this book to the three of them.

Table of Contents

Introduction

Introduction

"I'll find somebody new and baby we'll say we're through. And you won't matter anymore."
—Buddy Holly

The government has launched a number of bailouts and stimulus programs in recent years, sending trillions of dollars down the drain.

Like many, I am angry. Washington and Wall Street are tied at the hip and spend most of the time talking only to each other. They are connected socially and economically and have media outlets devoted to promoting their philosophies.

Wall Street and Washington are not having a positive impact on my world.

The public is outraged about out-of-control bonuses and out-of-control lobbyists, and I keep waiting for someone on Wall Street and Washington to get it. I am starting to think they never will. Politicians make gestures to keep us from rioting, but as soon as our backs are turned, Wall Street goes right back to its old ways.

Wall Street and Washington developed the saying "too big to fail." The idea is that big institutions must stay in business, no matter how badly they screw up.

The Soviet Union operated on the same premise.

Wall Street and Washington do not understand that entrepreneurs and small-business people have been the force behind economic growth the past few decades.

Advances in technology have made it possible for smart people who live in Kentucky, Oregon, India, and China to compete with any business Wall Street has to offer.

This trend toward small, entrepreneurial businesses that are located far from money centers isn't going away. Yet, Washington keeps throwing countless dollars at these "too big to fail" money losers.

After the Depression, we learned a lesson and put a variety of regulations in place. After the Depression, banks were relegated to banking and insurance companies were relegated to writing insurance policies. That worked well for more than fifty years. Then deregulation became the hottest fad and gave us companies such as Enron and many others.

In the modern world of deregulation, Citibank, a bank, was allowed to merge with Travelers, an insurance company. The new company, Citigroup, had to suck down billions in bailout money to survive. This "too big to fail" business model is not bringing us any advantages.

One reason Main Street gets overlooked is we don't know anyone in Washington or on Wall Street, and we really don't want to. Main Street's customers are local, and a lot of them, including me, deal with local and regional banks that know them and their businesses.

If Wall Street understood their customers, they would not have spent billions on credit default swaps and mortgage-backed derivatives.

People who start their own businesses don't need bailouts. Businesses in a startup phase aren't in need of tax cuts. What small businesses need is cash flow, access to capital, mentors, and guidance.

But, above all, they need the proper mindset. People who work for large companies expect their employers to look out for their concerns. Entrepreneurs are willing to look out for their own concerns.

After years of massive layoffs and cuts in employee benefits, workers at many corporations realize that their companies don't care about them. The corporation's only concern is making Wall Street happy. With big companies continually cutting back and jobs at large corporations becoming scarce, many people are now looking at entrepreneurship.

As Bob Dylan said, "When you ain't got nothing, you got nothing to lose."

I started my structured settlement and insurance consulting business at age twenty-three. I had finished most of my graduate work at Vanderbilt University, but the only job I could find was on the cleanup crew at the Kentucky Horse Park.

Cleaning up after horses will make you rethink your career options.

Starting my own business was a good move. January of 2013 will mark my thirtieth year in business. Both of my daughters and my son-in-law work with me.

There are two goals behind *Wealth Without Wall Street*. One is to give people ideas for improving their economic lives. The second is to take power away from Wall Street and Washington so they can't do all the horrible things they have done for the past thirty years.

My personal goal is to help you gain financial control as an individual but also to remind you that your actions will have an impact on the world.

The phrase "think globally, act locally" is overused, but it is a good principle to follow. Consider how Gandhi and Martin Luther King made such a big mark on society: They inspired individuals to take small steps that collectively made a huge difference.

Wealth Without Wall Street can be summed up in five steps:

1. Tear up your credit cards. Eliminate debt. Stay away from the "legalized loan sharks" such as payday lenders. I have not had a personal credit card in more than a decade. It's easier than you think.

2. See if you have what it takes to start your own business. Some people do and others don't. If you are self-motivated, you can make a huge difference for yourself and society by owning your own business. I'll give you a number of ideas on how to get to the top and stay there.

3. Get rich slowly. One of the great, but overlooked, books of the past twenty years is *Getting Rich Slowly: Building Your Financial Future Through Common Sense* by William Spitz, the former treasurer at Vanderbilt University. I morphed a number of his ideas about money with my own philosophies to help people develop plans for the long haul.

4. Move your money from a "too big to fail" bank to a bank or credit union in your community. I've been a contributing writer to the Huffington Post since 2008 and give credit to founder Arianna

Huffington for creating the ever-growing "Move Your Money" movement.

5. "Think globally, act locally" is what *Wealth Without Wall Street* is all about. By the end of the book, you'll have a road map for doing both.

—Don McNay, CLU, ChFC, MSFS, CSSC
Richmond, Kentucky

donmcnay.com or wealthwithoutwallsteet.org

Credit and Credit Cards

The Case Against Credit Cards

After watching many people get in trouble with credit cards, I've concluded that most Americans are better off without them. Credit cards not only charge outrageous fees and interest rates, but they also tempt people into decisions they wouldn't make if they were paying in cash. They are one of the quickest ways to fall into debt, and I no longer have one.

People use credit cards for a number of reasons. They are easier to obtain than a traditional bank loan. A lot of people, especially in a bad economy, use them to make essential purchases—such as food and clothing—when they are unemployed with no savings or are waiting for their next paycheck. I have not had a credit card in nearly a decade but did use them to keep my business running when clients were slow to pay me.

Credit cards are also used for unexpected expenses, such as medical treatment, auto repairs, or replacing a major appliance. They often fill the role of safety net when someone doesn't have a savings account to fall back on. But people also frequently use them for convenience, to travel, to rent a car, and to dine out.

I frequently espouse my no-credit-card view on talk-radio shows, and people will passionately debate my stance. They defend their own use of credit, noting they pay off the balance every month. Those who think they always pay their balance need to review their statements from the past two years to make sure it's true. Usually, they'll find an occasion or two where they slipped up. Sometimes that slip-up lasts for years or decades. Like an extra piece of cheesecake that stays on your hips for the rest of your life, credit-card debt can stay with you until death.

My primary reason for promoting a "zero credit cards" lifestyle is I know how easy it is to get in trouble with them. When I had them many years ago, they allowed me to justify impulse decisions. I am extremely overweight and would rationalize bumping from coach to first class on a crowded flight when I had a credit card handy. Not having a card has made it easier to resist temptation.

And, it's not only me. Studies have shown that people will spend 47 percent less at a retailer or restaurant if they use cash instead of a credit card.

I am a big fan of online shopping, but I do it with a debit card. That means I have to have the money in the bank to cover my purchase. My cards are issued through Visa and MasterCard and can be used anywhere a credit card is accepted.

A popular misconception is that renting a car or traveling without a credit card is impossible. I've traveled extensively throughout the United States and Canada using only a debit card. I've spent two decades in a "preferred" category with Avis because I rent cars so frequently.

As noted, you need to have enough cash in the bank to cover your purchases, and usually the rental car companies want a little extra in your account to cover any unexpected expenses. (Hertz asks for $200.)

More people have realized they can survive without credit cards, as evidenced by a Javelin Research study that found credit card use among consumers dropped 31 percent between 2007 and 2009. With the economic crisis, many people started cutting up their plastic as credit card companies increased interest rates and added fees. A lot of these companies also tightened the screws, cutting credit limits and cutting off high-risk customers.

That doesn't mean that credit card debt is going away anytime soon. As of May 2011, Americans had $793.1 billion in revolving debt, 98 percent of which is held on credit cards. The vast majority of Americans (176.8 million people) have credit cards. Those individuals averaged more than three different cards per person. Cardweb.com says that the average American household with one or more credit cards has a balance of $10,700, with interest rates that run in the high teens. The average combined total debt for all major credit cards increased by $20 from the first three months of 2011 to $4,699 per borrower. Even so, that amount is down more than 5 percent from the $4,951 average in the second quarter of 2010 and is 16 percent lower than the peak average debt of $5,575 in the first quarter of 2009.

When people get a credit card, they are not only putting themselves in a position to be charged high interest and fees, they also are giving up a huge amount of privacy. No one knows more about a person than your credit card company. Credit card companies know how and where you spend. They know what times of the year you need extra cash and in which situations you might blow your budget. You provide them that information every time you use your card.

In *A Piece of the Action: How the Middle Class Joined the Money Class*, Joseph Nocera wrote about Andrew Kahr, who got Household Finance, a consumer lending company, into the credit card business. Kahr had a knack for using mathematics and marketing techniques to find customers who would never pay off 100 percent of their credit card balance. His companies made a fortune, and Kahr retired at a very young age.

So how do you get credit cards out of your life?

In my structured settlement business, clients come to me with large lump sums, perhaps received from an inheritance or a settlement from a lawsuit. I tell the ones with credit card debt, "I don't offer any products that will pay you as much in interest as you are paying the credit card companies." I get people to pay off their debts, cut up their cards, and use the money they were paying to the credit card companies for savings or possible investments.

But, most people don't have piles of cash lying around and aren't counting on a big lump sum. Getting out of credit card debt is a slow process where you need to have a long-term goal.

Dave Ramsey and I disagree on several topics, but we agree on the goal of jettisoning credit card debt. I have attended Ramsey's live seminars and watched him explain his "snowball theory" for eliminating credit card debt. It works as follows:

Ramsey says you should pay off your smallest credit card first. Until the balance is eliminated, pay only minimums on other debt while focusing on the one credit card. This creates a momentum in your plan.

To quote Ramsey: "The math seems to lean more toward paying the highest interest debts first, but what I have learned is that personal finance is 20 percent head knowledge and 80 percent behavior. When you start knocking off the easier debts, you will start to see results and you will start to win in debt reduction."

I ran into a childhood friend at my mother's funeral who later told me she was maxed out on several credit cards. She is a clerical worker who doesn't make a lot of money. I told her about the snowball theory, and she followed it. She also cut back on impulse shopping. It took four years, but last year she e-mailed and told me she had paid off all the cards. Not only was it a great financial accomplishment, it dramatically boosted her self-esteem to know she could accomplish a seemingly impossible task.

My friend faced up to her financial dilemma. A lot of people get overextended, fall behind on payments, and start getting calls from credit-card collection companies.

If you have ever had a collection agency call you at work, or while a date is visiting your apartment (I've had both happen), it is a humbling and embarrassing experience. My credit card problems occurred before I had a mobile phone, but I would imagine getting a collection call on your cell phone with others around can't be fun.

People who are being hounded by collectors need to get familiar with the Fair Debt Collection Practices Act. It's been around for a long time but is widely ignored by banks, collectors, and regulators. It provides consumers with real protections when used correctly.

You can find a detailed booklet about the Fair Debt Collection Practices Act at www.ftc.gov/bcp/edu/pubs/consumer/credit/cre27.pdf

Few people realize (and collectors will never tell you) that if they want no further contact with a collector, the Fair Debt Collection Practices Act gives them a way to make the calls and letters stop. Collectors cannot communicate with consumers in any way (other than litigation) if the consumer gives written notice that he wishes no further communication or refuses to pay the alleged debt. With or without written notice, collectors can only contact consumers by telephone between 8 a.m. and 9 p.m. local time. Collectors cannot call repeatedly or continuously. Consumers can prevent collectors from contacting them at work simply by telling them not to. The consumer does not have to send a letter.

Collectors cannot contact consumers who are known to be represented by an attorney. Collectors can't use deception, such as implying they are an attorney or law enforcement officer, to collect a debt. They can't threaten arrest. They can't threaten legal action if it is not actually contemplated and they can't use abusive or profane language when speaking to a consumer.

Collectors routinely ignore the Fair Debt Collection Practices Act. They realize that few consumers know the law and fewer will complain. They also realize that the Federal Trade Commission, especially in the years before the 2008 market crash, rarely enforced the law.

I once had a collector (who was looking for a relative who had never lived in my city or household) violate almost every provision of the Fair Debt Collection Practices Act in a profane-laced rant. I documented the conversation in detail, filed a complaint with the Federal Trade Commission, and thought that such a clear-cut violation would get the agency's attention. It didn't. I got a form letter saying it would add my complaint to its files for statistical purposes.

Despite my unhappiness with the enforcement of the law, knowing it and citing it to collectors can often blunt abusive collections practices. Ending a string of harassing phone calls gives consumers time to deal with debts in a rational and well-thought-out manner.

After people get the creditors off their backs, they should sit down and devise a strategy for getting credit cards out of their lives.

Credit Card Company's Influence in Washington

The high mark for credit card companies in Washington came in 2005 when Congress modified the law to make it difficult for people with credit cards to discharge their liabilities by bankruptcy.

Considered a legislative victory for banks, the bill was denounced by consumer advocates. Long-time federal bankruptcy judge Joe Lee and author Thomas Parrish wrote in a January 13, 2007, New York Times opinion piece, that "In adopting the provision, Congress disregarded the advice of every disinterested group that has looked at the question, including three presidential commissions, the Congressional Budget Office, and the Government Accountability Office. It also ignored a past House Judiciary Committee report, which declared that such compulsion might well amount to the imposition of involuntary servitude."

Credit card companies again flexed their muscles in 2009 by watering down a consumer protection bill, the Credit Card Accountability Responsibility and Disclosure Act. Senator Christopher Dodd, who sponsored the legislation, stated that bank lobbyists were successful in keeping Congress from capping credit card interest at 36 percent.

The bill, signed into law by President Obama, requires that card companies give cardholders forty-five days' notice of any interest rate increases. The act has some good provisions that protect college students. It prohibits anyone under age twenty-one from having a credit card without a co-signer or without proof that they have the means to repay. It makes it harder for credit card companies to participate in college campus events, and outlaws giving away promotional items, such as free T-shirts and pizza, to entice people to sign up for cards.

The card act forces credit card issuers to offer lots of consumer disclosure (which few consumers actually read) and prohibits banks from some outlandish behavior, such as using misleading terms and due-date gimmicks.

I've yet to meet the person who uses credit cards as a way of achieving financial security. Although I know that the majority of people have credit cards and some are able to use them in a responsible manner, I advocate avoiding them.

Is Credit An Evil Thing?

I hate certain types of credit. I don't own a personal credit card, and I don't want one. Payday lending, tax-refund anticipation loans, and other forms of legalized loan sharking should be outlawed.

Too many people get in trouble with these "services" and with upside-down car loans, second mortgages, and high-interest-rate financing for home improvements and furniture.

I don't do any of them. None of my employees has a car loan. We don't buy brand-new cars, but we do buy nice, used ones. I drive an eight-year-old Lexus that I have had for six years.

Meanwhile, I have a nice house, with a low-interest mortgage and plenty of equity. I saw the downturn coming, so I lived in a rental house for four years and waited until I got a good deal.

I almost didn't do it. Getting a loan wasn't easy (I didn't have a credit history but could make a good down payment), and I don't like the idea of having any kind of debt.

Credit keeps many people from living within their means. At the end of their lives they wind up broke and struggling. I never want to be one of those people.

Many of my successful friends share the same philosophy about debt. They want as little as possible.

About the time I was thinking about purchasing a home, a friend told me he was buying a large house. This buddy is a financial genius. He is someone you have never heard of—and he wants it that way. I go to him for great insights, but he never lets me quote him.

He drives a modest car and lived in a modest home, both of which he paid for in cash. He is more interested in his portfolio than in pretense. He is a self-made success.

He said that with the housing market depressed and interest rates below 5 percent, it made good financial sense to buy a nice house and finance it for fifteen years.

I'm not sure he really wanted a nicer house. He just saw it as a financial opportunity.

He is rarely wrong and never makes irrational moves. It made me think again about the evils of credit. There are times when credit is good, such as when it is used responsibly by people who can handle it.

Take, for example, those in a high tax bracket who are financing houses.

If they borrow the money at 5 percent annual interest, the actual cost, in most cases, will be roughly 3 percent, after taxes. If they invest the money they borrowed in an immediate annuity, they would have the cash flow to pay the mortgage, get the mortgage interest deduction, and benefit from any increase in value of the house. (I am assuming that sometime in the next fifteen years, houses will appreciate in value again.)

In the meantime, the mortgage and annuity payments would stay the same.

That is a fairly low-risk way to use credit.

Someone could also put his money in the stock market and make big gains. Or lose his shirt. There has been a lot of shirt-losing during the past couple of years.

Investing in the stock market can be like going to the racetrack. There are going to be winners and there are going to be losers. People should understand that any investment involves risk.

In the subprime "too big to fail" anything-goes market that brought on the financial crisis, some people forgot about risk. Those are the people who should not have credit. None at all.

Many are tying themselves to lifelong debt by paying outrageous fees and interest on credit cards. Credit cards can charge 20 percent to 30 percent a year in interest plus really outrageous fees. Guaranteed. And you don't get a tax deduction. I can't think of a worse investment than that.

I watched so many people fall off the wagon on credit cards that I bought into the "just say no" philosophy on credit.

A pioneer in the "never borrow money" philosophy was Christian author and lecturer Larry Burkett. In the mid-1970s, he founded a nonprofit organization called Christian Financial Concepts, which used biblical principles in guiding people with their finances. One of those principles was no debt whatsoever.

Burkett, who died in 2003, was extremely popular in Christian financial circles, but he never reached a mainstream audience. Dave Ramsey has. He has a syndicated radio show and had a nightly program on the Fox Business News Network. In his book, *Financial Peace,* Ramsey acknowledged Burkett's influence.

Like Burkett, he focuses his attention on churches and Christian communities, but Ramsey goes on to reach every demographic. His message of savings and sacrifice and of never borrowing money is one that many people need to hear.

Then I think about my friend. His new home was a smart financial move.

Credit in moderation can be good. But like any addiction, credit can be the worst nightmare of your life.

It's safer to say "no" than to be tempted.

Payday Lenders: Legalized Loan Sharks

The town where I grew up in Northern Kentucky was a haven for organized crime. My father was a bookie and professional gambler who worked in several of the area's "hot spots."

In a town full of hustlers, prostitutes, and gamblers, the profession looked down upon most was loan sharking.

It wasn't unusual for a loan shark to wind up floating in the Ohio River. One of the biggest names in the business, Frank "Screw" Andrews, a central character in journalist Hank Messick's nonfiction book, *Syndicate Wife: The Story of Ann Drahmann Coppola*, "accidentally fell" out of a fourth-floor window.

If Andrews were in business today, he would be a captain of industry. Loan sharking has been legalized, in the form of payday lenders.

The stock of payday lenders is traded on the New York Stock Exchange and NASDAQ. Many payday lending companies do business with Wall Street's biggest banks.

As Gary Rivlin notes in his outstanding book *Broke USA*: "[T]he working poor have become big business."

You wouldn't think that poor people would be a growth market, but businesses make big money off people who live paycheck to paycheck.

There is a whole segment of society that does not use traditional banking services. They cash their paychecks at Walmarts, liquor stores, and payday lenders.

Andrews met his fate when he tumbled out of that hospital window in 1973. I'm sure when he fell he never dreamed that nearly forty years later his business would operate legally in almost every city in the country.

Andrews knew how to bribe local officials with cash payments. He didn't live to see such bribery legalized in the form of lobbying and political fundraising.

Broke USA makes it clear that the public and those in the media don't care for payday lenders, much the way the prostitutes and hustlers didn't.

The poverty industry has made huge contributions to lawmakers. According to the Citizens for Responsibility and Ethics in Washington, payday lenders donated more than $1.5 million to federal office holders during the 2010 election cycle. Substantial donations were made to state and local lawmakers as well.

Until I read *Broke USA*, I didn't realize what a big hand the "too big to fail" banks have in creating the poverty industry. Many payday lenders would not exist if Wall Street had not given them the money to get started.

Citigroup, JP Morgan Chase, and Bank of America are among the big banks that make huge profits, directly or indirectly, from the poverty industry.

The banks that fund the poverty industry have another common bond. They received bailout money from the American taxpayers in 2008.

If there was ever a shining example of why you should move your money from Wall Street, legalized loan sharking is a good one.

The people peddling poverty products realize there are Americans who are the financial equivalent of drug addicts. They will pay any price, fee, or interest rate as long as they can get an immediate fix. They don't care about tomorrow. They just want money today.

Another insight *Broke USA* provides is that many people use payday lenders because they don't have access to traditional banks. I didn't realize that many banks won't allow people with bad credit to open a checking account.

Since the alleged "financial reform" that Congress passed in 2010, banking services for lower-income people are getting worse.

"Too big to fail" banks are charging fees for checking, raising the minimum balance required for free checking, and hitting consumers with a bunch of nickel-and-dime charges.

Those nickels and dimes will add up to billions in profits for the banks we bailed out in 2008.

In reaction to financial reform, the head of JP Morgan Chase, James "Jamie" Dimon, seemed to speak for all of Wall Street when he told the New York Times, "If you're a restaurant and you can't charge for the soda, you're going to charge more for the burger."

The burger is going to come out of the hides of the banks' poorest customers.

As payday lenders and others in the poverty business have found, it is easy to stick it to poor people. They have the fewest options.

More and more of them will fall out of the traditional banking system altogether.

Financial reform is a boon for people in the payday loan business. When people fall out of the world of traditional banking, they still need bank-like services. Payday lenders will be in position to fill the gap.

Gary Rivlin and I have become friends since I did a review of *Broke USA* for the Huffington Post. We both agree that payday lending is not going to go away unless the government steps up to the plate to regulate it.

In 2006, the U.S. Department of Defense realized that soldiers had a problem with payday lenders. The department found that 17 percent of all military personnel were using payday loans, and soldiers' financial stresses were hampering their ability to function while fighting in Iraq and Afghanistan.

It was estimated that payday lenders were charging members of the U.S. military interest rates between 360 percent and 720 percent. Congress cut it to a maximum of 36 percent.

Despite losing the military market, payday lenders showed they still had plenty of clout. Congress could have easily extended that 36 percent cap to all Americans, but it did not.

Instead, the battle has become one each state must fight individually.

I suspect if you let everyone vote on the issue, payday lenders would go away quickly.

Broke USA detailed an Ohio referendum that capped payday lenders at 28 percent. The referendum got 63 percent of the vote. The route Ohio took is a roadmap for other states trying to do the same thing.

Unfortunately for the people fighting payday lending, most states don't offer ballot initiatives and referendums. They elect legislators and ask them to represent us.

Many of the groups fighting payday lending are part of larger coalitions with a litany of other legislative interests. Fighting payday lending is merely one of many issues on their plates.

Payday lenders have a well-organized, well-financed front, and they are going to fight with everything they've got. They make lots of contributions to all the right people and hire the best lobbyists.

What everyone needs to realize, though, is that this issue affects all of us. Wealth cannot be sustained over the long term when the poorest of a community are exploited.

Self Employment

Should you try the world of self-employment?

Tom Peters, co-author of *In Search of Excellence: Lessons from America's Best-Run Companies*, noted in a 1993 column titled "A Return to Self Reliance" that self-employment is not a new concept in the United States.

Peters wrote that 50 percent of Americans were self-employed in 1900 but that by 1977 the figure had dropped as low as 7 percent. By the time Peters wrote his article, the figure had gained a little ground, hovering at 13 percent.

According to the U.S. Small Business Administration (2009 statistics), we are now back to a point where roughly half of those employed in the United States own or work for small businesses.

Most Americans understand this. A paper written by David Blanchflower, an economics professor at Dartmouth College, said that 70.8 percent of Americans preferred to be self-employed as opposed to being an employee. In other countries such as Japan, France, and Great Britain, the number is closer to 40 percent.

If Americans like the idea of self-employment and know it presents the greatest opportunity for growth, what is stopping some of them from taking the plunge?

Many factors. Most obvious are lack of capital, education, skill sets, investors, and opportunity. People who are working double shifts at their existing jobs don't have time to start a business. Others do not handle money or free time well.

People often come to me when they are thinking about self-employment. I ask three essential questions, the answers to which tell me more than reams of data or business plans.

1. Are you cut out to be self-employed?

2. Do you have a dream you are working toward?

3. If you have a good job, should you leave it?

Are you really cut out to be self-employed?

Few people are suited to be their own bosses. Most people want a regular work routine. Their lives are based on forty-hour work weeks and steady paychecks. When people tell me they want to start their own business, I ask them whether they can really live without regular income.

I tell them to talk to their families and get their honest answers. I ask them whether they could go weeks or months without money coming in and how they would deal with it.

They need to understand they are trading their steady paycheck for an unsteady paycheck.

Many people want their own businesses for the wrong reasons. Like in the Alan Jackson and Jimmy Buffett song, *It's Five O'clock Somewhere*, people decide they don't like their jobs and that it would be fun to be self-employed. They don't realize that self-employment means it is never five o'clock anywhere.

I've told many professionals they should not go into business for themselves. They may be good workers with good ideas, but they couldn't handle the stress of not having a guaranteed income.

Never being off work can be hard on families. A friend of mine tried being an independent financial planner. He worked a lot of hours, and his wife started calling his office in the evenings. She put their children on the phone to tell him how much they missed him.

He went back to a steady paycheck at a big insurance company. He has less independence, but he is still married.

Some people become self-employed because no large organization will hire them. I did not plan to be self-employed, but I could not find a job out of graduate school other than cleaning up at the Kentucky Horse Park in Lexington. After I started my financial business, I realized I needed the independence of being self-employed more than I needed a steady paycheck.

Education and upbringing are important in deciding whether a person can make it as an entrepreneur. I was with Barbourville, Kentucky, attorney Sam Davies when a woman told him she was sending her son to military school. "He will learn how to follow the rules," she said. Sam replied, "He would be better off if he found a school where they taught him how not to follow the rules."

Sam, who never had a partner until his son Samuel joined him a few years ago, is one of the best attorneys in the United States, in my opinion. Most great trial lawyers practice by themselves or with a few associates. Few are in large firms. The attitude that makes them unafraid to take on billion-dollar businesses makes it impossible for them to fit into big corporations.

They produce an "unsteady paycheck," and they never know when five o'clock rolls around. Or Saturday or Sunday, for that matter.

Before a person decides on self-employment, he needs to figure out how important a steady paycheck and a steady calendar are in his life.

Do you have a dream you are working toward?

I primarily work as a structured settlement consultant. My clients are injury victims, lottery winners, and others who are receiving large sums of money.

Somewhere along the way, I stumbled on a way to get them to tell me about their deep-seated financial dreams.

I call it the lottery question.

I ask every person the same thing, "Forget about what is going on today. If you won the lottery, how would you spend the money?"

The initial answers are usually vague, such as "invest" or "put money in the bank."

Then, I tell them that when I become a billionaire, I am going to buy the Cincinnati Reds. When I tell them about my lifelong dream, they often start talking about the things that interest them.

From a planning standpoint, the lottery question is a great one. Everyone has dreams and desires but usually keeps them hidden in the recesses of his or her mind. The lottery question gets those dreams and desires out in the open, on the front burner.

Once we start the conversation, the list gets longer and longer. My goal is to get people to think long term. They need to clear their minds of everyday life's rat race. The lottery question makes that happen.

Everyone getting ready to start a business really needs to ask themselves the lottery question. Why are they doing it? What is the long-term goal? Do they plan on being in the new business the rest of their lives? Are they looking to make money or do other things, such as make an impact on society? If money is the goal, what do they plan to do with it after they make it?

When people look in the mirror and truly answer those questions, then they can decide whether they should start their own businesses.

Few Americans really think long term. Many people go through life without developing real goals or good habits. We need a lottery question to help guide the people in Washington and Wall Street. Those of us on Main Street need it, too.

Someone once said that American business people think quarter to quarter, Japanese business people think decade to decade, and Chinese business people think century to century. We've watched short-term myopia destroy Wall Street. We need to take a lesson from our friends in the Far East.

Should you quit the job you have?

The Johnny Paycheck song *Take This Job and Shove It* was a big hit because it resonated with a lot of people. They hate their jobs. They would take another job tomorrow if it had the same pay rate and economic opportunities.

Other people don't have the opportunity to quit. My friends in the newspaper business are being laid off in rapid fashion. Most of them never planned on doing anything else and do excellent work. Changes in how people consume news and some really bad corporate decisions impacted their careers.

But if you have a secure, well-paying job, you have to look at some obvious economic factors. Can you afford to quit? If so, for how long? Do you plan to use your 401k or retirement money to help start your new business? Although it is a common strategy, there are tax considerations and the chance you might run out of money in your old age.

I've met a lot of younger people who quit a job, lived on the 401k money for about a year, and then couldn't find another job. They were left with no money and a large tax bill to boot.

(When you make a 401k withdraw, you are taxed at ordinary income rates on the money you receive. Then, depending on your age and situation, you could get hit with a 10 percent tax penalty on top of that. I warn people not to do a 401k withdrawal unless it is absolutely their only option.)

The workplace is the social hub of many Americans' lives. My mother was an operating room nurse for twenty-seven years, but a workplace injury ended her career about ten years before she had planned to leave. All of her friends worked at the hospital, and being cut off from them pushed her into a depression that lasted several years.

Her situation is more common than people think. A number of my professional friends have retired and then un-retired because they missed their friends and routines. Also, some people are married to their jobs. They don't have hobbies or outside interests. Those people need to forget about a severance package and stay put.

I had the unique experience of helping many with the question of whether to take a buyout when the IBM plant in Lexington, Kentucky, became Lexmark in 1991. IBM had offered employee severance packages. People could take the package or take a chance that Lexmark would keep them on.

Several IBM employees came to me for advice. Many of them were engineers or had backgrounds in statistics. They wanted an answer they could quantify, so they sought me to calculate the present value of their package.

After thirty seconds of crunching the numbers, I asked the essential question: "What are you going to do with the rest of your life"?

Some had well-thought-out plans. They wanted to do charity work or start a second career. Others didn't. Working at IBM was not just a job; it was a lifestyle. They had never thought about life outside the corporation.

IBM employees were like a large family. They had generous benefits and perks. Most socialized with other IBM employees. People who went to work at IBM generally stayed for life. The idea of leaving the company was painful.

Companies that offer severance packages are generally established companies that sell the concept of lifetime employment. I've found that people leaving old-line companies, even with severance packages, are more bitter than those who work for companies that treat employees like interchangeable parts.

If you work at a company with high employee turnover, getting fired is not a total surprise. People at a company such as IBM never thought about working anywhere else.

Keep in mind that some severance packages are lucrative and offered on a one-time basis. I've seen people pass up a buyout and have their company go down a few years later. People often think their own industry is healthier than it is. It is good to get an objective opinion.

If your company is downsizing, find out whether severance compensation or insurance benefits are offered if you leave. If so, find out the amount of compensation. If you are receiving company health, life, or disability insurance benefits, ask whether those benefits will continue and for how long, then ask yourself if you can afford to pay for them on your own.

Severance pay is not an entitlement. Unemployment insurance is the only benefit that an employer must provide by law. Even if your employer has been generous in the past, that could change. The Wall Street Journal noted that prior to 2011, Pfizer gave departing employees three weeks' pay for every year of service. It then dropped to two weeks' pay for every year of service.

If an employer files bankruptcy, severance pay is rarely offered.

Some employees, especially those represented by unions, have employment contracts that specify a severance pay package.

There are employers who offer severance but demand employees give up any right to sue or file grievances as a condition for receiving the benefits. This is frequently the case when harassment, discrimination, or a hostile workplace environment has been alleged.

The Consolidated Omnibus Budget Reconciliation Act of 1985 (COBRA) gives departing employees the right to continue their group health insurance benefits for eighteen months after employment ends. The former employee has to pay premiums that an employer may have fully or partially subsidized, so it can be extremely expensive to maintain COBRA coverage. A more affordable option may be to join a spouse or domestic partner's insurance plan.

It is not uncommon for a person to stay in a job they don't like in order to have health insurance and other employee benefits. Legislation designed to make health care more accessible and affordable passed Congress in 2010 but will not to be implemented until 2014.

Wall Street is one of the few places where severance packages are still a common practice. Upon departure, top executives usually receive stock options, cash bonuses, and generous insurance benefits. Even executives who run companies into the ground sometimes receive generous severance. According to MSN Money, CEO Chuck Prince left Citigroup in November 2007 with a pension, stock awards, and stock options worth a total of $29.5 million. On top of that, he was entitled to a year-end bonus of $12 million. He also got an office, a car, and a driver for five years.

As Prince announced his resignation, Citigroup announced it would suffer more than $8 billion to $11 billion in losses due to subprime loans. A year later American taxpayers bailed out Citigroup. Prince was not required to pay back any of the benefits he received.

Main Street severance pay is much different. As noted, many businesses offer none at all. Others will offer lump sums, such as $1,000 a month for each year of service. Companies sometimes pay for the departing employee's health insurance for a limited time.

The time you may see a lucrative severance package in a Main Street environment is when a major company, with highly compensated and (and usually unionized) workers, wants to downsize its work force. A good example is Ford Motor Company. In 2009, it offered a buyout plan to all 41,000 employees represented by the United Auto Workers (UAW) union in order to get them to leave their jobs.

Employees who wanted to leave were offered $50,000 in cash and the choice of a $25,000 voucher to buy a vehicle or $20,000 more in cash. Enhanced early retirement was offered to employees fifty-five or older.

Although receiving a cash payout or severance may be the opportune time to look at a new career, I warn people who get lump sum packages not to make any sudden or stupid financial decisions. When severance plans are offered, hucksters come running, pitching everything from financial products to fast-food franchises.

Which leads to my final thought about starting your own business: Find a business you know. Lots of people make money running restaurants or franchises, but the failure rate is high, especially if you have never done it before.

I love being self-employed, and after doing it for thirty years, I can't imagine doing anything else. I encourage people who fit the profile to look at self-employment. I also encourage people who don't fit in the corporate world or who are out of work to seriously consider self-employment.

As Tom Stanley pointed out in *The Millionaire Next Door* and several of his other books, millionaires normally don't make their money investing in Wall Street stocks. They own Main Street businesses; they are building contractors, electricians, and plumbers.

My next-door neighbor is a plumber. I don't know if he is "the millionaire next door," but I know he has a beautiful home, a great family, enjoys his work, and has all the business he can handle.

He is a better definition of success than anything Wall Street has to offer.

The Second Act: Learning from your initial success and failures.

"And once you're gone, you can never come back."
—Neil Young

"There are two tragedies in life: One is not to get your heart's desire. The other is to get it."
—George Bernard Shaw, *Man and Superman* **(1903), act 4**

I learned during my first few years in business exactly what Shaw was talking about.

I hit it big at an early age. I started my business at twenty-three, and by twenty-nine I was one of the top producers nationally of mutual funds, annuity, and bond sales for the New York broker with whom I was affiliated.

I had achieved the highest levels in the Million Dollar Round Table. I had a huge house in an upscale, gated neighborhood, a red Mercedes Benz convertible, and a big, penthouse-style office on the top floor of one of Lexington's taller towers. I was featured in Forbes and Financial Planning.

One year later both my lawyer and accountant recommended that I file for bankruptcy. My net worth had plummeted far into the red, and banks were breathing down my neck. My business was still going strong, but I had gotten into a real estate deal that I didn't truly understand with people I didn't know well. And, it happened at a time when the market suddenly turned south.

Initially, I had grown my business by reinvesting profits and being frugal. I had lived modestly and had no debt. I knew my business backward and forward and spent a ton of money educating myself and my staff.

Suddenly, my cash was drained by a sideline investment and the expensive lifestyle I had decided to adopt. I didn't have the money to properly reinvest in my business and in continuing education. My focus went from a long-term view to just getting through the day.

I made the classic mistake of a successful entrepreneur. I thought my first success meant that I would be successful at everything. I got away from the things that had gotten me to the top.

If you study the history of entrepreneurs, you'll see that many do what I did. Their initial idea works. They become successful but then get distracted with outside interests and start to lose the single-mindedness that made them a success. Some recognize their mistakes and regain their focus. Others do not and their businesses fail.

I was lucky. I was able to see what I did wrong and make corrections.

The year was painful, but I learned lessons I will never forget. The experience was as valuable as a Harvard MBA, and I paid more than the school's tuition to achieve it.

In order to get back on track, I had to go back to my roots like Rocky did in the movie *Rocky III*. I had to regain the "eye of the tiger."

I thought long and hard about what I needed, what I wanted, and the mistakes I had made. I sat near the lighted, uphill waterfall in my massive house, looked at my beautiful car, and realized the house and car weren't important. The only creature comforts I needed were an ice maker, cable television (this was pre-Internet), a recliner, and air-conditioning.

What I really valued was financial independence and the challenge to be the best at what I did. I couldn't be independent if banks, creditors, and a fancy lifestyle controlled my life. A line in Bill Hybels' book, *Christians in the Marketplace: Making Your Faith Work on the Job*, hit me. It essentially said "if you spend all your time making money to support a material possession like a car, the car has replaced God in your life." Or as the band Zoe Speaks said several years after Hybels, "If money's our God, I want a new religion."

My religion had become keeping up my lifestyle and managing debt. Once I realized what I really valued—financial independence—it was easy to implement a different plan.

I ditched the big house and traded in the Mercedes for a Buick. I relocated my panoramic office to a small one on a ground floor. I sold most of the furniture in my home, except for the bed and recliner, and moved to a modest apartment that had air-conditioning, an ice maker, and cable.

I read and reread *Pizza Tiger*, the biography of Tom Monaghan, the founder of Domino's Pizza. Monaghan's career path had the same sudden boom and sudden bust before he finally broke through to an international level. I couldn't afford to buy the book so I kept checking it out of the public library. (I own two copies of it now.) Monaghan's story gave me hope and inspiration.

I eventually knocked out my debt as I reinvested in my business and education. I got a second master's degree in financial services and my fourth professional designation.

Going back to the original formula got me on a growth path again. Four years after I ignored the advice to file bankruptcy, I was out of debt and my business was bigger than ever.

"Stick to what you know" seems like common-sense advice, but I have watched many business people make the same mistake I did. Once things start to go well, entrepreneurs think success will last forever. They often get into ventures outside of their expertise and start spending too much money and time on a fancy lifestyle.

When they crash, they do one of two things. They give up and quit or they "double down," to use a gambling term, and focus harder on the original business. Like Monaghan did with Domino's Pizza. After he doubled down, his company reached success beyond his wildest dreams. He made millions, enough for him to buy the Detroit Tigers baseball team.

As I made my comeback, I used to play an obscure Jim Croce song, *Age*, every single day. Two lines were my mantra. "And now I'm in my second circle and I'm headed for the top, I've learned a lot of things along the way. I'll be careful while I'm climbing because it hurts a lot to drop."

Some of the lessons I teach throughout the book, such as moving your money to a local bank and not having a boatload of debt, were learned through hard and painful experiences. Experiences I want others to avoid.

When people hit it big, they need to stick to what they know, live below their means, avoid credit cards and loans, and put some money away for a rainy day.

Otherwise the first act can be a final act.

Getting Rich Slowly

Getting Rich Slowly

My approach toward wealth changed in 1992 when I went to a Vanderbilt University alumni meeting and heard William Spitz, the college's treasurer, give a talk about his book, *Get Rich Slowly: Building Your Financial Future Through Common Sense.*

In the book, Spitz sums up his philosophy in ten principles:

1. There are no guarantees, sure things, or free rides.

2. It is not necessary to earn extraordinary rates of return to accumulate a sizeable net worth. Earning consistent, reasonable returns while avoiding losses should be the focus.

3. Structure your program to understand the risks involved and have faith in your program to ride out the tough times without making hasty or costly decisions.

4. Diversification is crucial. Spread your risk.

5. Index funds will usually do as well, or better, than investment advisers or managed mutual funds.

6. Make decisions based on economic performance and not on tax avoidance.

7. Have the same program for asset allocation, no matter how much or how little you are investing. A person with $5 million to invest would split it into multiple types of investments; so should the person with $5,000.

Wealth Without Wall Street

8. Every investor is his own worst enemy. No one is immune from swings in emotion and from following the herd. Structure your finances to avoid the availability f sudden decisions.

9. Minimize costs whenever possible.

10. Too much trading and moving money is expensive and counterproductive. To quote Spitz, "The primary beneficiary of a high level of trading is your broker." Set up your portfolio carefully, review it annually, stick with the plan, and don't panic.

Get Rich Slowly: Building Your Financial Future Through Common Sense is aimed at academia and is not an easy read, but for me it was an epiphany. I had similar thoughts about how to make money, but Spitz summed them up in one book. It has been the cornerstone for all my philosophies since then.

Spitz gave his advice sixteen years before the Wall Street crash in 2008. People who had their money allocated as Spitz suggested— among a variety of stocks, bonds, mutual funds, real estate, and annuities—did much better in 2008 than people who had put their eggs in one basket.

A lot of people, including many at Wall Street banks, thought real estate could never go down. They put all their money in the real estate market and got burned.

When I worked as a Series 7 registered representative (often referred to as a stockbroker), I followed the lessons of the *Get Rich Slowly* book religiously. I had a large clientele of doctors, lawyers, and other well-educated professionals, along with injury victims and the occasional lottery winner.

I had my clients allocate their money into several types of investments and did my best to keep them from panicking when one class of investments did poorly. I reminded them it takes time to "get rich slowly."

Over the years, I kept noticing one thing. People who had easy access to cash were the ones most likely to fall off the "get rich slowly" bandwagon. They would have "emergencies," such as buying a new car or a houseboat, or taking their friends on a cruise. Sooner or later, the money would be gone; well before they were able to "get rich slowly."

In the meantime, I had a parallel business that provided structured settlement annuities to injury victims. Structured settlements are only offered to injury victims and are tax-free. Thus, they are an attractive choice compared to taxable alternatives.

A structured settlement annuity can be designed in a number of ways, but the way I normally recommend is to pay it out over a person's lifetime, increasing it at 2 percent or 3 percent a year to keep up with inflation, and in case the recipient dies, guaranteeing it for thirty years to a beneficiary.

One of my first clients was a young man who lost his arms and legs in an accident and received roughly $3 million. If he and the motorcycle gang with whom he lived had gotten their hands on $3 million, they would have had the party to end all parties until the money was gone.

I set up an annuity so he received $10,000 a month.

Thus, they had a party every month until he died many years later.

You can't really cash in a structured settlement although some people make the unfortunate decision to sell their payments to companies like J.G. Wentworth, which heavily advertises on television. (If you watch daytime television such as the Jerry

Springer Show, you are likely to see Wentworth or one of its many competitors.)

Because the money was harder to access, the people who took structured settlements were more likely to "get rich slowly" than my professional clients who could cash in a mutual fund or stock whenever they wanted.

I finally realized it was like dieting. I struggle with my weight in a big fashion and usually start a diet about once a month. If I start a diet when I have all my favorite foods in the refrigerator, I will fall off the diet immediately. If I have to drive to the store about two miles away, I think about it more and sometimes won't go. If I have to drive twenty-five miles to get fatty foods, I am far more likely to stick to the diet.

The financial analogy is that having all your money in a savings or checking account is like having food in the refrigerator. Putting money in a mutual fund or certificate of deposit, where it takes some effort (and sometimes penalties and tax consequences) to cash it in, is similar to driving to the store two miles away. A structured settlement is like the twenty-five-mile drive for food. You have to do a lot of work to sell it and take a huge financial hit when you do.

It is better just to hang onto the structured settlement and stay disciplined, just like it is better to stay on a diet.

Eventually, I moved away from a successful career as a stockbroker and focused all my efforts on the structured settlement business.

Although many of the eggs are in the structured settlement basket, it was closer to the Will Rogers philosophy of being concerned about "return *of* my money as opposed to return *on* my money."

There is something similar to a structured settlement called an immediate annuity. It pays income for a person's life, just like a defined benefit pension plan. Although people seem to like lifetime income from a retirement plan, a Smart Money article stated what I long suspected: Few people buy them on their own.

I never understood why until I read an article called "The Annuity Puzzle" in the June 4, 2011, edition of the New York Times.

Dr. Richard Thaler, a professor of economics and behavioral science at the University of Chicago Booth School of Business, discussed how using 401k retirement funds to purchase an immediate annuity, with fixed and guaranteed benefits, was a simple and less risky option than self managing a portfolio or having the people on Wall Street do it for you.

He also noted that few people do it.

Thaler suggested that people seemed to consider an annuity a "gamble" that they would live to an old age instead of realizing that "the decision to self manage your retirement wealth is the risky one."

As people live longer than previous generations, they are more likely to run out of money before they run out of time on the earth.

An annuity is just one tool, like balancing your money among a number of different investments, but the key to "get rich slowly" is to develop good savings and spending habits. A person can't get rich, quickly or slowly, if he spends more than he makes.

He also will never be in a position to acquire financial independence or wealth without Wall Street.

The Case for Consulting with an Attorney

"Send lawyers, guns and money."
—**Warren Zevon**

Every year since 1991, the Gallup Organization has polled Americans on which profession they consider the most honest and ethical. When nurses are on the list they always come out on top, except in 2001 when firefighters, understandably, took the distinction.

Lawyers always run near the bottom, ahead of lobbyists, car salespeople, and members of Congress but behind reporters, bankers, and auto mechanics.

Love them or hate them, if you plan to make money, and keep it in the family after you die (or if you want to make sure your favorite charities get some cash), you need to develop a relationship with an attorney. It will save you a lot of grief in the long run.

Lawyers can help you with business disputes and tax questions. They can make sure your business and real estate purchases are set up correctly. Lawyers can help you plan what happens to you or your family if you should suddenly die or become disabled. And, even more important, they can make sure those plans are carried out. Lawyers can help if you are in an accident. They can help if you are being sued or jerked around by creditors. Lawyers can help if someone owes you money and won't pay.

I've watched people make serious life decisions without using lawyers. That usually doesn't work well. I've seen people pay unnecessarily large chunks in taxes (usually along with penalties and interest) because they didn't ask a lawyer about a transaction. I've seen property disputes arise that didn't need to happen, simply because people didn't use attorneys to draw up proper deeds, leases, and agreements.

One such dispute stirred up so much acrimony between neighbors that one shot and killed the other. (The shooter then hired a lawyer to represent him in the murder trial.) I've watched people negotiate accident settlements with insurance companies and get far less than a good trial attorney would have gotten for them.

I've seen people get burned because they drew up employment contracts or business agreements without an attorney to help them. I've watched people, sometimes extremely wealthy people, lose everything because they co-signed or guaranteed loans and didn't ask an attorney to guide them through the pitfalls.

Often when a person avoids using an attorney, he winds up hiring one later to straighten out the mess. It's like the last time I tried to fix my car without a mechanic. I turned a $50 problem into a $500 one.

I encourage people to use an attorney when they start their own business. I hope the same people become so successful that they eventually need tax and estate planning attorneys to set up trusts to protect their assets and fund worthwhile charities.

When it comes to finding a good lawyer, I have a strong bias toward Main Street lawyers over Wall Street lawyers. (If you are totally stumped and can't find the kind of attorney you need, e-mail me at don@donmcnay.com, and I will refer you to some.)

Main Street lawyers deal with common problems and common people. They tend to charge Main Street fees instead of Wall Street fees. I'm tired of subsidizing Wall Street lawyers who go to Washington and "regulate" the people they used to work for. A blog by Matt Taibbi of Rolling Stone magazine about the practice was titled: "The SEC's (Securities and Exchange Commission) Revolving Door: From Wall Street Lawyers to Wall Street Watchdogs." Taibbi said that one Wall Street firm, Wilmer Hale, had so many employees leaving the firm to join the SEC or leaving the SEC to join the firm that the firm was nicknamed "SEC West."

The dynamics of a small town are perfect for developing skills that make someone a top-notch lawyer. Small-town juries won't allow the stunts pulled in the O.J. Simpson trial. The juries won't tolerate a lot of flash and showboating.

In a small town, everyone knows everything about everybody. It's like a scaled-down version of Facebook, except you don't get to choose the news that is posted.

It's the type of continuous oversight that would greatly benefit Wall Street.

Most of us need someone to double check decisions and keep us from making serious mistakes.

That is the thing that lawyers do well.

My Story—Why People Need Wills

"Everything we got, we got the hard way."
—**Mary Chapin Carpenter**

I've spent my adult life advising people about their money. I've worked closely with many lawyers. I'm extremely knowledgeable about trusts and estate planning and have strong working relationships with experts in both fields.

I have a will. I tell anyone who comes in my door to get one. No matter how old or young, rich or poor, I tell them they need a document that will specify what happens with their assets when they die.

With my background and experience, I should be the last person to be involved in an estate-planning nightmare. But I was when my mother and sister died.

Mom had a brain aneurysm and died unexpectedly on April 2, 2006. She never had a will, and no one ever really worried about it. Her only asset was our childhood home, and my sister and I were her only children. We would split the ownership of the house equally.

Only, things got a lot more complicated after Mom's death.

My sister and her twelve-year-old daughter were living in the house when Mom died. My sister was coming off a period of unemployment in California as a single mother. She had no money. She didn't even have a bank account. She had just gotten a great job at Proctor and Gamble and was getting back on track after her years in California, which had drained her.

I was hit for a lot of estate expenses the moment that Mom died. I paid for her funeral, and I advanced the estate money to pay delinquent property taxes, some outstanding bills, and the mortgage on Mom's house. I couldn't borrow money against Mom's house (it was owned by the estate, not me), so I had to pay the expenses from my personal assets.

My sister and I worked out a deal. When the estate settled, we would get an appraisal and I would buy the house at the appraised cost. After I mortgaged the house, I could get back the money I had advanced to the estate. Her share of the house equity would give her cash to rent the house from me until her daughter graduated from high school. That would give her time to save up and buy the house from me and keep it in the family.

We never wrote anything down, but we trusted each other, and it seemed like a good plan. And it was—until my sister fell down a flight of steps and died in October 2006. She did not have a will, either.

I knew she had a minor child and an adult son. What I didn't know was that she still had a husband.

She had been married to this man for several years, and her younger child was his. However, she had told us she had divorced him several years earlier. They didn't live together and, for most of that time, she had lived in California and he had lived in Cincinnati.

He came to her funeral, which I had arranged and paid for, and though he said hello, we didn't really talk.

Two days later, he had a lawyer file papers asking that he be named the estate administrator.

I hired a lawyer and found another to represent my nephew (he had a different father), saying that my nephew should administer her estate.

After exhaustive research, it turned out my sister and her husband never filed for divorce. Thus, under Kentucky law, her husband was entitled to half of my sister's estate. My nephew and niece would split the other half.

Since Mom's estate had not settled, it also meant that her estranged husband and his lawyer (after several rounds in court, he and my nephew were named as co-administrators) suddenly became involved in decisions regarding my mother's estate. Also, my niece was a minor, and a guardian ad litem had to be appointed to protect her interest. The guardian ad litem (an attorney appointed by the court) also had to sign off on decisions about Mom's estate.

It was a tedious and expensive mess.

The only way to reach a solution was to put my childhood home on the market. I advanced another chunk of money to get it fixed up for sale. Since the real estate market was dropping, the house was slow to sell, and every time we wanted to change the price, it had to go through the round of lawyers and interested parties for approval. An offer early in 2007 was turned down. That offer turned out to be more than what the house finally sold for in December 2007.

The arguing back and forth caused a riff in the family over very little money. By the time the lawyers and other expenses (I got back the money I advanced) were paid, my share of my mother's estate was a small sum and my sister's estate received the same.

A bill from an attorney came in after Mom's estate had settled. I was so tired of dealing with everything that I paid it myself rather than reopening the estate. Thus, I lost money on the overall process.

The person who got the most money from my mother's estate was my former brother-in-law. My sister's estate received half of Mom's money, and he received half of my sister's estate. My nephew and niece split the other half of her estate.

My mother doted on her grandchildren, especially my sister's children, who had lived with her for part of their childhoods. She would not have wanted my brother-in-law to get that money instead of her grandchildren. And preventing that from happening would have been easy and inexpensive.

My family's series of events was unusual, but unusual things happen every day.

Involving a lawyer would have solved most of the problems. If my sister and, especially, my mother had had simple wills, the process would have been smoother and the money would have gone to the right people. If my sister had actually gotten divorced instead of working out an informal agreement (my brother-in-law was good about paying child support), it would have prevented our post-funeral surprise.

Losing a family member is difficult. It is unfair to ask the people left behind to make decisions and guess at the deceased's intentions. Also, state laws don't always reflect a person's true intentions and have to be honored in the absence of a will providing differently.

I suspect people don't have wills because they don't want to think about death. According to a survey by Findlaw.com, a popular legal website, more than 60 percent of Americans don't have wills. As the Findlaw site notes: "A will is a basic component of estate planning. Among other things, it specifies how your assets will be distributed after you pass away, and who will receive them. Without a will, the laws of the state and the decisions of a probate court may determine how your estate is distributed, who will care for your children if they are minors, and so forth."

In her book *Living Richly: Seizing the Potential of Inherited Wealth*, Myra Salzer cited a 2003 study of 3,250 wealthy families and said that 70 percent of all wealth transitions fail. I suspect it's because people did not write a will or set up a simple estate plan.

According to the Findlaw survey, only 25 percent of people between twenty-five and thirty-four have a will; fewer than 10 percent of people in the eighteen to twenty-four age bracket have one.

People over fifty are more likely to think about wills. More than half of the people that age have them. As noted, my sixty-seven-year-old mother did not.

I knew someone with terminal cancer who waited until a few days before his death to make a will. He just couldn't deal with it before then. I've been told about another situation where an attorney supposedly had an agreement about what would occur in the event of his death, but when he became terminally ill and waited until the last minute to try to get those partners to confirm the deal in writing, they suddenly had no recollection of any such agreement.

People may think that wills and attorneys are expensive. In the overall scheme of things, they really aren't. I gladly would have paid ten times the average cost for my mother and sister to have had wills. And everyone (but my brother-in-law and the attorneys) would have come out way ahead.

It's time to talk about insurance, even if you don't want to.

As people work to make money on Main Street, insurance plays a key role in making sure that an illness, fire, or accident does not put them out of business and that the financial goals for families and charities are met if the person who set the goals dies before they are achieved.

I've been affiliated with the industry for twenty-nine years. All of the titles behind my name—Chartered Life Underwriter, Chartered Financial Consultant, Masters in Financial Services, Certified Structured Settlement Consultant—have some relationship to the insurance industry.

I'm a licensed life insurance agent in several states and a licensed life and health insurance consultant in Kentucky, which means I can charge a fee instead of taking a commission for my advice. I'm also a licensed claims adjuster in Kentucky. Dealing with insurance claims is part of what I do in the structured settlement business.

I understand the power of life insurance.

The first life insurance check I ever delivered was for a twenty-eight-year-old family friend who was hit by a truck. The money allowed his family to bury him, hire a lawyer, and eventually win a verdict against the trucking company.

A year later, the second death claim I filed was for my father, a fifty-nine-year-old who died of prostate cancer. I had argued with him for years before he agreed to buy the policy. He hated insurance and didn't really like it being part of my career path.

Near his death, he thanked me for convincing him to get the coverage.

I became a true believer in life insurance after Dad's death.

That makes me dramatically different from Main Street America.

According to the Wall Street Journal, "The number of individual life policies sold annually in the U.S. dropped 45 percent over the past twenty-five years, even as the number of households with children rose more than 25 percent. Meanwhile, the number of $2 million-plus policies, typically sold to affluent households, has been rising."

Wealthy people, who can afford first-rate advisers and attorneys, see the need for life insurance, but the message is not getting to Main Street.

I have theories as to why.

I've met a lot of quality insurance agents—really bright people who care about their clients and recommend innovative solutions. I've become acquainted with many of them through the Million Dollar Round Table, an association for financial professionals who meet standards of excellence.

No one beyond their individual clients knows much about them.

You don't see many reality shows about insurance agents.

If you asked the average person to describe a typical insurance agent, he would come up with a character such as the one Bill Murray kept punching in the movie *Groundhog Day*: a pushy, not-so-bright person who is more interested in making a sale than helping his clients.

I've been lucky to know people who have devoted their lives to the insurance industry and really know their stuff. Insurance advisers play an important role in people's lives, and agents should have the same kind of extended credentialing process and rigorous continuing education required of certified public accountants.

Some companies are seriously resisting this push for professionalism, especially Primerica, which has one of the largest sales forces in the country. Primerica was part of Citigroup when taxpayers bailed it out in 2008. It spun off in 2010, with Citigroup holding a stake in the new company.

According to an April 25, 2011, Wall Street Journal article: The people at Primerica think life insurance tests are too *hard*! Meanwhile, the company depends largely on part-time agents, whom the article said "don't actually become insurance agents, often because they flunk state licensing exams, according to filings and interviews." About 80 percent of the 230,000 Primerica recruits in 2010 didn't become insurance agents, often because they failed the exam.

The perception of agents is one hurdle. Another obstacle is that the industry does not have a natural leader or public figure who stands out in the public's mind the way Steve Jobs at Apple or Bill Gates at Microsoft do. Warren Buffett is a big player in the insurance industry, but the public views him as an investment guru.

The most recognized figures in the insurance industry have one thing in common: None of them are human.

Few Americans can identify the president of any insurance company anywhere (I've been in the business twenty-nine years and can only name a few), but most Americans can identify the GEICO Gecko, the AFLAC Duck, and Snoopy from Peanuts, who advertises Met Life.

When an insurance company is faceless or is represented by comic figures or silly commercials, it is easy for it to be defined by negative stereotypes and bad claims practices.

Having an experienced and educated insurance adviser can make a huge difference. People can find good agents in almost every city in America. If not, the next town down the road will have one.

People need to choose an adviser based on professionalism and credentials not because the agent plays golf or sings in the church choir.

I'm not crazy about the health insurance industry. Premiums are high, and for years I did pitched battle with them over claims and exclusions. Since I am a licensed health insurance agent, for many years I sold myself my own health insurance.

It was like a doctor operating on himself. A bad idea.

I finally asked a longtime friend who specializes in health insurance to help me. He has qualified for the Million Dollar Round Table for more than forty years and has a boatload of education.

Since I started letting his firm handle the benefit planning for our business, the claims battles have gone away and, in the past year, our premiums decreased.

As I said at the beginning, it's time to learn more about insurance. The best place to get that education is from a well-trained insurance professional.

Move Your Money

The Case For Moving Your Money

"Hey I think the time is right for a palace revolution but where I live the game to play is compromise solution."
—The Rolling Stones.

Most of us have an idea of what a small-town banker should be like. It's George Bailey, the character Jimmy Stewart played in *It's a Wonderful Life*.

We also have an idea of what a Wall Street "too big to fail" banker might look like. It's Gordon Gekko, the character Michael Douglas played in *Wall Street* and the sequel, *Money Never Sleeps*.

Although everyone wants to bank with George and no one wants to bank with Gordon, people keep winding up at Wall Street banks.

According to FDIC data from 2009, 57 percent of bank assets are with the top twenty banks. Thirty-eight percent of bank deposits went to the five largest banks, up dramatically from 1994 when only 13 percent of deposits went to the big five.

Why?

Big banks spend big money on advertising. The website Business Insider War Room combed through the annual reports of publicly traded companies and found that JP Morgan Chase spent $2.4 billion on advertising in 2010. Bank of America spent $1.9 billion, and Citigroup spent $1.6 billion.

The billions being spent in advertising would seem to casual observers to be the overwhelming factor in attracting customers, but that doesn't appear to the case.

My friend New York Times opinion columnist Joe Nocera wrote an award-winning book, *A Piece of the Action*. Joe tracked the evolution of personal finance in America, including the credit card and banking industries. He cited research that said people picked their bank primarily because of its convenience to where they live or work. No other feature mattered. Very few consumers shopped for better interest rates, lower fees, or better services.

Little has changed since Nocera wrote his book in 1994. A 2008 Compete.com survey asked 1,600 people who banked online about online and offline activities. The survey found that 52.6 percent gave "convenient location or ATM" as the reason they chose their bank. Less than 20 percent gave bank fees as the reason. And, despite the billions being pumped into advertising, only 6.3 percent said they chose their bank based on that factor. Since Bank of America has 18,000 ATMs and 6,233 branches, more than any other bank, it would make sense that it attracts the most deposits.

Based on the data and history, getting people to move their money from a Wall Street bank to a possibly less-convenient local bank would seem like an uphill challenge. But, at the beginning of 2010, Arianna Huffington, co-founder of the Huffington Post, and some of her friends decided to take on that challenge by creating the "Move Your Money" project.

According to a December 29, 2009, article that Huffington and economist Rob Johnson wrote for the Huffington Post (disclosure: I have been a Huffington Post contributor since 2008), the idea arose at a pre-Christmas dinner they attended with political strategist Alexis McGill, filmmaker Eugene Jarecki, and Nick Penniman of the Huffington Post Investigative Fund. The group discussed "what concrete steps individuals could take to help create a better financial system."

They started with a website and a video. It has grown from there. According to Sara Ackerman, coordinator for the Move Your Money project, more than 4 million people moved their money away from Wall Street banks in 2010. Michael Moebs, CEO of the economic research firm Moebs Services, said that between 13 million and 17 million people will move their money from Wall Street to a community bank or credit union by the end of the project's third year (2012).

There are some practical reasons for consumers to move their money. Moebs Services research shows that overdraft fees in 2009 averaged $35 for large banks compared to $25 for small banks. A similar gap existed with bounced check fees and stop-payment orders.

Personal service is another point in favor of small banks. According to J.D. Power and Associates (and quoted on the moveyourmoneyproject.org website), "small banks have consistently rated higher in overall customer satisfaction than their Wall Street counterparts and that gap has only widened in the last few years."

Supporting small business is another benefit that Move Your Money touts. According to FDIC data, 57 percent of bank assets are with the twenty largest banks, but only 28 percent of small-business lending comes from that top twenty. Small banks (defined as under $1 billion in assets) provide 34 percent of the loans, and mid-size banks (assets between $1 billion and $10 billion) provide 20 percent of the loans.

Although data shows that moving money from a Wall Street bank has benefits for the consumer and for Main Street, a primary motivation for the Move Your Money movement is to decrease the power of Wall Street banks and their role in the financial markets.

It took $700 billion in taxpayer money to bail out Wall Street banks in 2008. Most of the losses for Wall Street came from casino-like trading in a financial instrument called derivatives. Few of the losses came from loans, deposits, or services traditionally done by banks.

It was more profitable for big banks to act as gamblers rather than as deposit and lending institutions. The quest for profits, documented in books such as *The Big Short: Inside the Doomsday Machine* by Michael Lewis and *Too Big to Fail: The Inside Story of How Wall Street and Washington Fought to Save the Financial System—and Themselves* by Andrew Ross Sorkin, set Wall Street up for a huge crash.

Wall Street banks have not learned much from their 2008 near-death experience. According to a report issued by the U.S. comptroller of the currency, in the fourth quarter of 2010, four of the biggest Wall Street banks held 95 percent of the derivatives for the entire banking industry.

In other words, JP Morgan Chase, Citigroup, Bank of America, and Goldman Sachs have 95 percent of the exposure to losses in the derivatives market. The other 6,349 banks in the United States have 5 percent.

It's stunning to see Wall Street banks go back into a derivatives market after being burned so badly. It's like watching someone jump out of a sixth-floor window, survive the fall, and go up to the eighth floor and try it again.

I want to send Wall Street a wakeup call, as they don't seem to be getting it or particularly appreciative that taxpayers bailed them out.

The best way to send that message is with my dollars. My resources don't add up to what a chairman of a Wall Street bank gets in an annual bonus, but keeping those dollars away from Wall Street is a start.

As more and more people join the Move Your Money movement, it will get Wall Street's attention. It's also an action that everyone can do. Even my eleven-year-old grandson.

Move Your Money has a tax-deductible 501(c) foundation that raises money to educate financial consumers. I made a contribution to the foundation and encourage others to do the same.

Make a donation, or learn more about Move Your Money, at http://www.moveyourmoneyproject.org.

Think Globally, Act Locally

Think Globally, Act Locally

"And I'm pulling out of here to win."
—**Bruce Springsteen**

I wrote this book for two reasons.

I've spent several years as a financial columnist and decades as a financial consultant. I wanted to put my common sense advice in a book that people could reference.

My goal is to help people avoid the school of hard knocks I attended. The tuition there was higher than at the prestigious universities I went to, but the lessons were more valuable. I want to share those lessons and save others the pain, money, and time of going through them.

The other reason I wrote the book was to give people a path that will decrease the influence of Washington and Wall Street on our lives.

Few in Washington listened to the people on Main Street who strongly opposed the Wall Street bailouts in 2008.

Somewhere along the way, Washington and Wall Street stopped talking to Main Street.

Part of the reason is that Washington and Wall Street don't feel economic pain firsthand.

I was in Washington during the lowest point of the economic crisis of 2008 and was struck by how different it was from other cities. Unlike state and local government employees, federal employees were not being furloughed or laid off. Lobbyists and consultants in Washington seemed to be fully employed. Washington real estate was not in freefall, like it was in Florida and Nevada. Washington remained one of the most expensive cities in the United States.

Washington couldn't have empathy with the pain of Main Street because they were in a totally different world.

People try to pinpoint when Washington and Main Street disconnected. I think it was in the 1970s, when paid political consultants became a dominant force in American politics.

Image-making has been part of presidential politics since 1840, when the wealthy and socially prominent William Henry Harrison defeated Martin Van Buren after Harrison was marketed as a "log cabin and hard-cider drinking" common man. Prior to the 1970s, in order to get elected, office holders had to maintain some tie to grassroots political organizations that drew their power from supporters on Main Street.

Professor Larry Sabato at the University of Virginia wrote an influential book, *The Rise of Political Consultants,* in 1982. Sabato discussed how technology such as political polling, targeted direct mail, and sophisticated media purchases allowed candidates to run for office without the support of a political organization.

A potential candidate didn't have to spend years knocking on doors, stuffing envelopes, and working his way up in a political party. All he had to do was raise enough money to hire well-trained consultants who could execute an image and a message that voters would buy.

To paraphrase Vince Lombardi, after the advent of political consulting, raising money wasn't everything, it was the only thing.

There is no easier place to find money than on Wall Street.

Washington could go to Wall Street and come back with sacks of money. Wall Street could get Washington to do things that would let it make more money. That meant Wall Street could increase the amount of campaign donations and lobbying money it sent back to Washington.

Robert Kaiser nailed it in his outstanding book, *So Damn Much Money: The Triumph of Lobbying and the Corrosion of American Government.* When Main Street differs with Wall Street, Washington will consistently weigh in on Wall Street's side.

Some people are looking for a political solution. I really don't see one. Measures such as public financing and campaign spending limits have been tried and ultimately shelved. Whenever a law is passed, political fundraisers eventually find a way around it. The result is that Wall Street keeps sending money to Washington.

I spent my post-college years heavily involved in politics. Most notably, I was a state coordinator for Al Gore's 1988 presidential campaign. I see many good people in elected office. Most get into public life wanting to make a difference. All of them eventually learn one thing: the art of getting re-elected.

People who spend their lives in elected office are very good at staying there. Just like you and me, they want to hang on to a career they worked hard to earn.

Congressmen understand what it takes to keep 51 percent of the voters happy and they are good at it. Since 1980 at least 80 percent of congressmen and 75 percent of senators were re-elected in every election cycle. Noting that trend, change in political leadership is going to be marginal at best.

No matter which political party is in power, Wall Street manages to have its own people on crucial congressional committees, in cabinet-level positions, and in almost any bureau that might attempt to regulate them.

The influence of big money on Washington is not going away soon. There is not a viable way to replace it.

I don't advocate marching in the streets or writing a letter to your congressman. Your congressman's pollster has already told him what you are thinking about before you even sit down at your computer or lace up your shoes.

A better form of protest is to set up your own finances in a way that reduces the influence of Washington and Wall Street on your life.

For many years, the two parties have been the Democrats and the Republicans. Now I view the parties as people who depend on Wall Street and people who don't depend on Wall Street.

My major suggestions are non-partisan in the traditional political party sense.

The idea of reducing debt and getting rid of credit cards is frequently advocated by conservative radio host Dave Ramsey. Being self-employed is a concept both political parties tout in some fashion. Move Your Money is a concept that Arianna Huffington, a Progressive, developed. Americans agree with the theory of "get rich slowly" and giving back to their community, even if they don't always practice the concept themselves.

The best way to think globally, act locally is to do two things at the same time.

Each individual can work toward being a good citizen. That includes supporting local businesses, being a good neighbor, and gaining financial independence.

Secondly, recognize that your actions can ultimately reduce the power of Wall Street and Washington over Main Street.

That is what "thinking globally, acting locally" is all about.

It is also what *Wealth Without Wall Street* is all about.

Epilogue August 2011

Epilogue: August 2011

The 2008 Wall Street bailouts were a defining moment in history, signaling a complete disconnect between Wall Street and Main Street.

I opposed the bailouts from the minute they were proposed.

My first concern was that bailing out Wall Street would not fix the root problem. Over the past few decades, Wall Street's focus went from providing capital to businesses, to developing products, to generating fees and large bonuses for a favored few. By propping up "too big to fail" banks with a bailout, though, we never allowed them to address the root problems that got them in trouble in the first place. As soon as they could get away with it, Wall Street banks went back to paying themselves million-dollar bonuses.

My second concern was that the bailout would delay a chance for a quick recovery. Japan went through a "lost decade" in the 1990s, where its strategy of propping up failing institutions prolonged its economic pain over an entire decade. Having seen what happened in Japan, it wasn't hard to predict something similar for the United States.

Without the Wall Street bailouts in 2008, the financial and real estate markets would have dropped by huge margins. Some "too big to fail" companies would have failed. Then, investors who had handled their money better would have bought up the bargains, created a bottom, and the economy would start rebuilding. In a short period, we would have been on the way to recovery.

That is how capitalism works.

The United States has had many booms and busts. Many people and companies have had ups and downs. Apple Computer was on the brink of bankruptcy in 1997. In August 2011, it surpassed Exxon Mobil Corporation to become the world's largest company.

People can come back from the bottom. They just need to know where the bottom is.

As I predicted in 2008, the United States has limped along economically for the three years since the bailout. On the week I am writing this, the United States had its credit rating downgraded below AAA by Standard and Poor's. It is the first time in history something like this has happened. Every sector of the economy seems to be in chaos. Washington has not addressed long-term issues such as how to pay for Medicare, Medicaid, and Social Security for an increasingly aging population. State and local governments have huge pension payments due for their retired employees, and few have put aside enough money to meet their obligations. The American unemployment rate is over 9 percent and the real rate of unemployment, when you count people who have stopped looking for jobs, is nearly twice that.

Many Americans are burdened with serious credit card, consumer, and student loan debts. Their houses are worth less than their mortgages, and a lot of them are wondering whether they will have a job tomorrow.

Americans are burdened with fear, the fear of not knowing when, or if, the hard economic times will end.

If we had skipped the bailouts, it would have been a horrible 2008, but I suspect it would have been a much better 2011. We would have cleaned up the problems and started all over again.

A primary reason for Main Street anger was the unfairness of the Wall Street bailouts. Wall Street did not suffer for its mistakes.

Goldman Sachs received bailout money (its former chairman and CEO, Henry Paulson, was Secretary of the Treasury during the bailouts) through its dealings with AIG, an insurance company that got an estimated $180 billion in bailout money. A chunk of AIG's bailout money went back to Goldman Sachs in an incredibly good arrangement for the most profitable securities firm on Wall Street.

Business owners know that if they screw up, they can go out of business. If I make a bad business decision, no one is going to bail me out.

Going broke doesn't scare me. If I hit bottom, I have the skill set to get back to the top. I've developed a knack for surviving adverse situations. As Jimmy Buffett said, "If it suddenly ended tomorrow, I could somehow adjust to the fall."

Most people on Main Street know they can come back. People on Wall Street never got a chance to see whether they could.

I don't want a government handout, but I don't want to pay for Wall Street to have one either.

The disconnect between Washington and Main Street is more than a breakdown in communications. We know that people on Main Street increasingly don't trust people in Washington. As I write this, a record 82 percent of Americans disapprove of the way Congress is handling its job.

Congress would fare better if its members weren't so busy pandering to special interests. They should be turning their energy toward mobilizing constituents with a shared vision for the future.

In his 1961 inaugural address, President John F. Kennedy urged Americans to "pay any price, bear any burden, support any friend, oppose any foe in order to assure the survival and success of liberty." He also said, "Ask not what your country can do for you—

ask what you can do for your country." Many people believed in Kennedy's aims of shared sacrifice and public service.

Kennedy set the seemingly impossible goal of having an American walk on the moon by the end of the decade. On July 20, 1969, it happened.

Americans aren't into shared sacrifice these days, maybe because no one has really asked.

We have seen Americans step up to the plate before.

After the attack on Pearl Harbor, Americans pitched in to win World War II. Although most able-bodied men volunteered for service, there was a draft for those less willing. Taxes were dramatically increased to fund the war effort. Supplies such as gasoline and food were rationed. People were challenged to put 10 percent of their savings in war bonds. Profiteers were prosecuted and put in jail.

That total sense of commitment resulted in Germany's and Japan's unconditional surrender. It spawned a group of people called the "greatest generation." Those Americans contributed to the greatest economic run in history when the war ended.

Americans had a golden opportunity to have that same sense of shared sacrifice in the week after September 11, 2001. After nearly 3,000 Americans were killed in a terrorist attack, the country was completely united. Partisan bickering seemed to go away, and we were ready and eager to pitch in to help.

If our leadership had called on the same sacrifices to fight terrorism that Americans made in World War II, such as imposing a draft, rationing, and increasing taxes to fund the anti-terrorist efforts, Americans would have gone for it.

It wouldn't have hurt to ask, but nobody did. A once-in-a-lifetime opportunity was missed to rally Americans to participate for the common good.

Until Washington gets the courage to trust the American people to handle hard and sobering decisions—and develops a plan of action that does not favor one interest group over another—real economic solutions are not going to come from Washington.

I don't see economic solutions coming from Wall Street, either. The purpose of Wall Street is to make money for the brokers and the shareholders. Period. The corporate raiders of the 1980s made a compelling point that anyone who was not interested in maximizing shareholder value needed to be replaced with someone who was.

It is not Wall Street's charge to solve larger economic problems, and at no point in history has it done that. As long as Wall Street holds on to the clout it developed in Washington, it will use its clout to maximize profits. That is what shareholders want.

The possibility of economic change is most likely to come from people on Main Street. The ideas that I outline in the book are practical and offer a lot of common-sense solutions for the individual. Implementing the ideas will make people more financially independent.

Financially independent people can handle the stress of economic chaos better than those who live near the edge. Some live near the edge because of poverty, lack of education, and lack of resources. Others live near the edge because of lifestyle. They spend more than they make, don't save, and don't have long-term plans.

I am not encouraging people to march in the streets, call into talk shows, or write their Congressmen. Economic action is more effective. If Americans set up their lives so that we depend less on

Wall Street and Washington, both entities will notice. We will be hitting them in the place where it hurts the most: their wallet.

With economic action as a primary tool, historic figures such as Gandhi and Martin Luther King were able to implement positive change on society. I want *Wealth Without Wall Street* to inspire that spirit of positive change for the United States in the year 2011 and beyond.

—Don McNay

Acknowledgments

In her book, *Hot (broke) Messes: How to Have Your Latte and Drink It Too*, Washington Post personal finance writer Nancy Trejos said, "Writing a book is like what I imagine a pregnancy would be like: You don't sleep well, you gain weight, you cry a lot and you constantly worry that there will be something wrong with the final product."

During the time I have been writing this book, my daughter Gena has been pregnant with her second child. My lot in life has been easier than hers but there have been days when I could relate to Nancy's statement. Writing a book is a test of endurance and persistence.

This being my third book, I learned to surround myself with a group of supportive and talented people. My name is on the cover but the book is truly a group effort.

I dedicated this book to my fiancée, Karen Thomas; my mentor, Al Smith; and my granddaughter Adelaide. They bring true love and joy to my life.

Adelaide was not alive when I wrote my last book, and I will have another grandson shortly after this book hits the market. I've been blessed with a wonderful family, and I dedicated my first book to them.

I adopted my daughters, Gena Bigler and Angela Luhys, after they were adults. I had been their stepfather for several years. Angela brought me my first grandchild, Abijah Luhys. Both Gena and

Angela have leadership roles at the McNay Group (www.mcnay.com), and my son-in-law Clay Bigler serves as company president. Some people hire a great organization. I adopted one and love them dearly. I appreciate how they have been able to keep the businesses rolling seamlessly while I have been out working on the book.

My nephew, Nick McNay, fulfilled my family's dreams when he graduated from Northern Kentucky University in May, and his expert videography skills are being utilized to do a series of videos about the book. I look forward to the day, a few years in the future, when my incredibly intelligent niece, Lyndsay Jo Francis, joins her brother in walking down a college graduation line. I just read an article featuring my stepmother, Lynn McNay, and how she is making a big impact in her adopted home city of Montgomery, Ohio. I dedicated my previous book to my mom, dad, and sister. I miss them every day. My own family will increase by three next year when I marry Karen. Her children—Max, Emily, and Zach Kirby—will be a great addition to my life.

Rena Baer's commitment to excellence shines through every page of this book. I made the decision to find a high-powered professional editor, and I hit the jackpot with Rena. Rena is an accomplished journalist and seasoned book editor, and you can read more about her at www.renabaer.com. Rena has been more than an editor. She has been a coach, friend, teacher, and inspirational leader, and she is totally confident of her command of the English language. Her organizational skills are incredible. She told me that she was not going to let me quit until I totally used all of my writing talents. She meant it. She has pushed me as hard as I can be pushed. I have rewritten chapters, sometimes seven or eight times, and chapters that didn't live up to Rena's standards were tossed out. She has dealt with impossible deadlines, my temperamental nature, my late-night phone calls (Rena does most of her editing in the morning; I do most of my writing around midnight), and has been a perfect counterbalance to my approach to writing. Thank you, Rena.

Rena suggested Vickie Mitchell as a second editor, and they make a great tag team. Kathryn Marcellino in Modesto, California, did the layout and book-cover design, and I appreciate her twenty-five years of experience and expertise.

Louisville lawyer Jeffrey Stamper has played a unique role in my life. Unlike Rena, who can quote from various stylebooks and note the nuances from one to another, I have not opened a stylebook since college, and it showed in several of my newspaper columns. Jeff wrote to me a few years ago and said the grammatical errors were driving him crazy and volunteered to edit my columns for free. I took him up on it, and he has done a terrific job. Jeff is a great lawyer and one of Kentucky's brightest minds when it comes to real estate and property law. I can see how his attention to detail serves him well as an attorney and appreciate all he has done for me.

Tiffany Clark Nash is coordinating my book tour. An accountant by training, Tiffany was the Republican nominee for state representative in my home city of Richmond in 2010, and I got to see her intellect, personality, and work ethic during that campaign.

The Web page and theme for the *Wealth Without Wall Street* organization was put together by Mary Ashley Burton, who worked for me in 2010. She wrote all the initial content for the site and produced a number of videos. I hired Mary Ashley as producer of my syndicated radio show. Two weeks before launch, the show was indefinitely delayed, and Mary Ashley shifted to a number of other projects. *Wealth Without Wall Street* was one of them. After she left, the idea sat on the shelf for several months until I was able to dust it off and bring it to life.

Mary Ashley's brother, Jordan Burton, designed the Wealthwithoutwallstreet.org website and the *Wealth Without Wall Street* logo on the front of the book. Jordan worked with Roy Stout at Stout Printing to develop a logo for the *Wealth Without Wall Street* stationery. Shortly after working with us, Roy was tragically killed when he was hit by a car while vacationing in Jamaica. Roy was a dedicated volunteer in the Lexington arts community, and he took seriously the concept of giving back to his community. RIP, Roy.

I've been fortunate to befriend some of the best writers in America. Gary Rivlin, Ed McClanahan, Byron Crawford, Suzette Martinez Standring, Al Cross, Judy Clabes, Samantha Swindler, and Rick Robinson honor me with their wonderful comments in front of the book and on the book cover. Joe Nocera, opinion page editor for the New York Times, is quoted several times in the book and has been a wonderful friend and mentor.

From the broadcast world, Renee Shaw, Jim LaBarbara, Joe Elliott, Tom Leach, Neil Middleton, Keith Yarber, and Len Press are friends whom I admire and learn from. I am honored by the wonderful comments from them and, also, from Len Blonder, one of the most influential people in the history of the structured settlement business. Len is a hardcore Los Angeles Dodger fan but is the opposite of former Dodger manager Leo Durocher's observation that "nice guys finish last."

Legendary Philadelphia columnist Stu Bykofsky said about my previous book that "if everyone you mentioned in the acknowledgements buys the book, you will have a bestseller."

I've attempted to shorten the acknowledgements (and hope the people mentioned in the previous book understand), but the following people deserve a shout out:

Pete Mahurin, Martha Helen Smith, Pierce Hamblin, Robb Jones, Ben Pollock, Bill Garmer, Greg Bubalo, Mike Behler, Dave Lieber, Connie Kreyling, Samantha Bennett, Lee Gentry, Larry Doker, Jamie Hargrove, Donna Davis, Ivan "Buzz" Beltz, David Grise, Tom Sweeney, Shelia Holdt, Brian House, Dr. Richard Vance, Kelly Wallingford, Peter Perlman, Richard Hay, Phil Taliaferro, Rhonda Hatfield-Jeffers, John Eckberg, Bess Byron, Rick Robinson, Carroll Crouch, Yvonne Yelton, Wes Browne, Debbie Fickett-Wilbar, J.T. Gilbert, Adam Collins, Nathan Collins, Randy Campbell, Sam Davies, Bob Babbage, Laura Babbage, Keen Babbage, Greg Stotelmyer, Carla Wade, Jack Brammer, Bob Haught, Stephenie Steitzer, Ferrell Wellman, Renee Shaw, Keith Yarber, Liz Hansen, Kevin Osbourn, Steve Carroll, Randy and Mary Beth Jewell, Arianna Huffington, Nick Penniman, Bonita Black, Lorie Love, Marisa Anders, Randy Patrick, Wendell Wilson, Alan Stein, Rob Dollar, Dr. Phillip Hoffman, Nancy Hoffman, Dr. Jim Roach, Carl Kremer, Chris Kremer, Judge Bill Clouse, Len Press, Lil Press, Ken Kurtz, Al Cross, John David Dyche, Lou Romanski, Gary Hillerich, Jim Todd, Bill Walters, Nick Lewis, Jodi Whitaker, my neighbors in the Waterford subdivision, and those other Kentuckians who, like me, are both an honorary Kentucky Colonel and a Duke of Hazard.

It doesn't get more Main Street than being a Duke of Hazard.

Finally, I have to thank Karen Thomas, and not just for being the woman I adore and for listening to my war stories for the past year. She encouraged me to restart the *Wealth Without Wall Street* project and to buck it up and listen to Rena (whom she has never met) on days when I didn't feel like redoing a page for the fourth or fifth time. Karen is a school principal and does not tolerate whining, complaining, or an effort less than 110 percent. There were days when I needed that kind of attitude to get the book finished, and I love her for it.

Don McNay, CLU, ChFC, MSFS, CSSC

Author, Syndicated Columnist, and Financial Consultant

www.donmcnay.com

Wealth Without Wall Street: A Main Street Guide to Making Money is Don McNay's third book. His previous books are *Son of a Son of a Gambler: Winners, Losers & What to Do When You Win the Lottery* and *The Unbridled World of Ernie Fletcher.*

An award-winning syndicated financial columnist and Huffington Post contributor, McNay has appeared on numerous television and radio programs in the United States and Canada, including the CBS Evening News with Katie Couric. He has been quoted in publications around the world, including USA Today and Forbes, Registered Representative, and Financial Planning magazines.

McNay was a pioneer in structured settlements, the field of helping injury victims and lottery winners handle large sums of money. He founded McNay Settlement Group, which is part of the McNay Group (www.mcnay.com), in 1983. He is considered one of the world's leading experts in structured settlements and qualified settlement funds. His company has been noted for its work with special-needs children, along with injury victims and lottery winners.

In 2000, McNay helped found the Kentucky Guardianship Administrators, which administers qualified settlement funds nationwide and serves as a court-appointed conservator for juveniles and incapacitated people in Kentucky. He is the owner of McNay Consulting and provides entrepreneurial advice for small-business owners. He is also a fee-based insurance consultant for individuals and businesses in Kentucky and a licensed claims adjuster.

A graduate of Eastern Kentucky University, McNay was inducted into the Eastern Kentucky University Hall of Distinguished Alumni in 1998. McNay has a master's degree from Vanderbilt University and a second masters from the American College in Bryn Mawr, Pennsylvania.

In 2011, McNay was named a Quarter Century Member of the Million Dollar Round Table, signifying that McNay met the organization's highly selective standards for service, production, and ethical behavior in twenty-five different years.

McNay has four professional designations in the financial services field.

Don received the Certified Structured Settlement Consultant (CSSC) designation from a program affiliated with Notre Dame University. He is a Chartered Life Underwriter (CLU), a Chartered Financial Consultant (ChFC), and earned the Masters of Financial Services (MSFS) designation.

Wealth Without Wall Street is not just a book; it's a primer for taking action.

"I have not yet begun to fight."
—John Paul Jones

"Let's give them something to talk about."
—Bonnie Raitt

I wrote this book to inspire Americans to take steps to improve their finances and their futures.

To support the effort, I launched the *Wealth Without Wall Street* website. You can find it at http://wealthwithoutwallstreet.org/. The page will educate and guide you as you work toward financial independence. It will also allow you to connect with others who have the same philosophy.

In addition, information can be found at www.donmcnay.com and on my *Wealth Without Wall Street* Facebook page at https://www.facebook.com/home.php#!/pages/Wealth-Without-Wall-Street/126445620737806, both of which are updated regularly.

—Don McNay